Wright Numbers

A North Carolina Number Book

Written by Carol Crane and Illustrated by Gary Palmer

A special thank you to Julie Wichard at the North Carolina Department of Transportation for providing photo reference for river ferries, and Mrs. Hanes Handmade Moravian Cookies of Winston Salem for photo references of cookies.
—*Gary Palmer*

Sleeping Bear Press

310 North Main Street, Suite 300
Chelsea, MI 48118
www.sleepingbearpress.com

THOMSON
GALE

© 2005 Thomson Gale, a part of the Thomson Corporation.

Thomson, Star Logo and Sleeping Bear Press are trademarks and Gale is a registered trademark used herein under license.

Printed and bound in Canada.

10 9 8 7 6 5 4 3 2 1

Library of Congress Cataloging-in-Publication Data

Crane, Carol, 1933-
Wright numbers : a North Carolina number book / by Carol Crane ;
illustrated by Gary Palmer.
p. cm.
Summary: "Using numbers many of North Carolina's state symbols, history, landscapes, and famous people are introduced. Topics include Pilot Mountain, Corolla wild horses, peanuts, and Scottish bagpipers. Each topic is introduced with a poem and detailed expository text"—Provided by publisher.
ISBN 1-58536-196-8
1. North Carolina—Juvenile literature. 2. Counting—Juvenile literature.
I. Palmer, Gary, 1968- ill. II. Title.
F254.3.C735 2005
975.6—dc22   2005005962

Special Note:

Wilbur and Orville Wright are the namesakes for the title of this book. Bicycle shop owners and tinkerers from Ohio, these two brothers first became interested in manned flight at the end of the nineteenth century. They built a glider and then looked for a place with the right winds to test flying. They chose the Outer Banks sand dunes, North Carolina. A camp was set up and experiments were started near Kill Devil Hills. For two years they set records for flying gliders. The Wright brothers were convinced a motor powered manned craft could fly. In 1903, they built such a craft and after many attempts, they were finally able to stay airborne for twelve seconds on December 17th. The Wright Brothers National Memorial was erected on the site of the first flight where visitors from all over the world can honor these two men and their contribution to history.

To my new North Carolina traveling companions, Eleanor and Vicki, Kevin Jayes, media specialist extraordinaire, and Tracy and Wilson Huntley, native North Carolinians who express the kind nature of this great state.

CAROL

❧

In loving memory of my father, number one in my book.
To my mother, for her faith and encouragement.
In memory of Mercer Wilson, friend, neighbor, storyteller.

GARY

Pilot Mountain looks like a giant mushroom on a rocky stem. It can be seen from 30 miles away on a clear day. The Native Americans called it "*Jomeokee*" or "Great Guide." Its two pinnacles soar up into the air and are connected by a saddle of rock and trees. The mountain was mapped in 1751 and became the 14th North Carolina state park in 1968.

In spring the mountains are radiant with bright pink Catawba rhododendron and mountain laurel. Rock climbing and rappelling are favorite activities at Pilot Mountain. Canoeing the Yadkin River, which runs through the park for two miles, is scenic and beautiful. The mountain has miles of hiking trails to explore. When hiking, it's wise to always look for poisonous snakes. North Carolina has 37 species of snakes and six are poisonous. They are the copperhead, cottonmouth (or water moccasin), eastern diamondback rattlesnake, timber rattlesnake, pigmy rattlesnake, and the eastern coral snake.

one

1

1 Pilot Mountain,
    a tall mushroom capped with green.
Pinnacles jutting upward,
    with a rocky bridge in between.

Telling us of days gone by,
a scene in our state's landscape;
2 old tobacco barns,
each with its own distinct shape.

Tobacco barns of every size and shape are seen throughout North Carolina. It is said they are part of the landscape. If these timeworn barns could talk, you would hear a history of farmers growing bright leaf tobacco. The tobacco barn is a symbol of the crop's importance to Tar Heel life.

Life on a tobacco farm was hard work for the entire family. The seeds were sorted, planted, and transplanted to another field. Too much rain, too much sun, or a hailstorm could ruin a crop. The leaves were picked by hand. They were then cured by a fire in the barns. When the leaves turned a golden brown, they were loaded onto wagons or trucks and sold at auction. The song of the tobacco auctioneer could be heard across the land at harvest time.

two

2

The Sans Souci Ferry hears a call from the other side of the river and starts up its diesel engine. Looking like a floating boat ramp, it chugs out into the river to pick up a customer on the other side. The Sans Souci Ferry and the Parkers Ferry cross the Meherrin River in Hertford County. The Elwell Ferry crosses the Cape Fear River in Bladen County. They are the last surviving trio of two-car and inland-river free ferries in North Carolina. None of the ferries are on state maps and are used by local farmers, residents, and visitors who happen to find them. The San Souci Ferry saves 20 miles for travelers who want to get to the other side of the Cashie River. The Parkers Ferry means a ride of a few minutes instead of a 15-mile drive around the river. These tiny ferries are a part of Tar Heel transportation history.

three
3

3 inland river ferries
hear the cars calling "toot, toot."
Riding across the river,
a short and fun route.

Living in the northern Outer Banks,
    descendants of Spanish mustang lore.
4 Corolla wild horses,
    surviving shipwrecks and swimming ashore.

Historical records show that Corolla's wild horses have lived in the northern Outer Banks since the early 1500s. They are descendants of mustangs that survived the wreck of a Spanish galleon (ship) and swam ashore on the Outer Banks. Today the horses no longer roam free. The development of the area has caused these majestic horses to be rounded up at the Currituck Beach Lighthouse and fenced in at the nearby Currituck National Wildlife Refuge.

A group of local citizens was concerned and took steps to secure the safety of the horses. The citizens erected a mile-and-a-half-long fence stretching from land to sea. The fence would allow the horses to roam freely, but safely. However, the horses had a mind of their own. Like sly children they waded out into the water on a sandbar and went around the fence to get back to the sweet grass they remembered. The Corolla wild horses have survived for more than 400 years. Development continues to endanger the future of these magnificent animals.

four

4

Basketball's inventor, Dr. James Naismith, was an educator and leader who believed in developing character through sport. The birth of the game was an assignment in his college physical education class. He worked out the rules for playing this new game: (1) no running with the ball, (2) no tackling or rough body contact, (3) there would be a horizontal goal above the players' heads, and (4) freedom of any player to obtain the ball and score at any time.

Dr. Naismith asked the janitor if he had two boxes 18 inches square. The janitor answered, "No, but I have two old peach baskets." So the baskets were nailed to the wall and used as goals. This is how the name of "basketball" was born. In December 1891 the first game of basketball in history was played in Springfield, Massachusetts. Michael Jordan is one of many famous basketball players that have graduated from North Carolina colleges.

five

5

5 basketball players on the court.
Women and men shooting hoops to win.
North Carolina's cheering fans,
supporting their teams again and again.

Our family is ready to go! We have on our gear. Grandma, Grandpa, Mother, Dad, my sister, and I are given safety instructions from the guides on what to do when whitewater rafting. The Nantahala River (pronounced nan-tuh-HAY-luh) winds through North Carolina's most scenic mountain terrain. We will travel eight miles on the river over all kinds of conditions. The journey will take three hours. When we reach the rapids, we go faster and faster. The rapids have names such as: isle of dumping, root canal, tumble dry, and fast ferry.

The Nantahala River is a dam-controlled river so the water level is just right all year long. Many families take the two-hour trip on the Great Smoky Mountain Railroad to go up the river and then raft back down the Nantahala. At the end of the trip, warm showers, dry clothes, and a lunch are waiting.

six

6

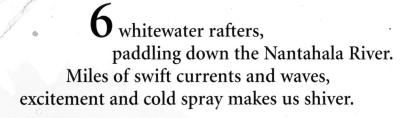

6 whitewater rafters,
paddling down the Nantahala River.
Miles of swift currents and waves,
excitement and cold spray makes us shiver.

The traditional folk mountain toy, known as the Gee Haw Whimmy Diddle, is the focus of a contest every year at the Folk Art Center in Asheville. The toy is made with two notched, wooden sticks and a paper propeller. The object of the game is to slide one stick against the other over the notches until the propeller turns. The winner of the contest makes his Whimmy Diddle propeller spin from left to right in the shortest amount of time.

Why is this toy called a Gee Haw Whimmy Diddle? It is a whimsical (whimmy) toy that you diddle (or play) with. In olden days, people trained their plow mules to turn right or left when they called out, "Gee" or "Haw." This is a rhythm toy and when keeping time to the music, men, women, and children of all ages get into the beat of the sticks.

seven

7

7 Gee Haw Whimmy Diddles—
an Appalachian toy from the past.
Rubbing two notched sticks together,
as we watch the propeller go fast.

These creatures are so prized in Transylvania County that in 1986 the Brevard city council established a sanctuary for all squirrels, especially the Brevard white squirrel. At first one might think they are albinos. However, naturalists have declared them indeed white squirrels. They have normal dark eyes, and albinos would have pink or red eyes.

These squirrels first appeared in North Carolina when they were gifts from a friend in Florida to a resident of Brevard, North Carolina. These wily squirrels escaped from their cages in Brevard while being fed and over time the population has grown. So if you are ever in Brevard and see a white squirrel scampering across a park lawn or climbing a tree, you are not seeing ghosts!

eight

8

Scampering up trees
8   what a ghostly surprise!
white squirrels.
I can't believe my eyes.

9 clay pots,
for planting our peanut seeds—
this year's science fair project.
Will our venture succeed?

North Carolina ranks third in peanut production in the United States. Peanuts are high in protein and vitamin B. They are low in sodium and have no cholesterol.

From the mid-1600s to the mid-1800s, Africans were brought to North America to work as slaves in the plantations. Peanuts from West Africa kept them nourished during the long voyage across the Atlantic. Once here in America, the Africans planted peanuts, along with corn, beans, and greens. The word "goober" (another name for peanut) comes from the Bantu African name for peanuts—*nguba*.

To grow your own peanuts you will need clay pots with a drainage hole in the bottoms, sandy soil, and raw peanut seeds. First, soak the seeds overnight, and then plant them one inch deep. Put the plants in direct sunlight, and keep the soil moist. Seedlings should sprout within five to eight days. Blooms should appear in 45 days. It usually takes three months for peanuts to appear on a potted plant.

nine

9

Blue crabs have **10** legs.
Watch out for their front claws!
It's best to leave them alone.
They have powerful jaws.

The blue crab is found along the Atlantic Coast. Its body is really olive-green, but its claws and legs are blue. The tips of its claws and its body spines are usually red, and its underside is white. The crab has five legs on each side of its body. The first pair of legs form the pincers. The next three pairs are walking legs, and the last pair that look like paddles, are used for swimming. If it loses a leg in a fight, the crab will grow a new one within two months!

The female crab lays two million or so eggs, but only a few will make it to adulthood. The female stays in the brackish (part salty, part fresh) water of estuaries until she is ready to release her eggs. Then she swims out to the open ocean to free the eggs. It is amazing that the blue crab can live in both fresh- and saltwater.

ten
10

North Carolina plays host to more tundra swans in the winter than any other state on the East Coast. Each year, 65 to 75 thousand swans migrate to northeastern North Carolina to take advantage of the many food sources found in lakes, farms, and bays. Male swans are called cobs; females, pens; and young swans, cygnets. As soon as the young hatch, they are ready to take to the water and paddle around.

The Atlantic Flyway Swan Research Project monitors the swans' habits. Using a tracking device around the swans' necks, the researchers track the route the swans fly in the spring and then their route back again in the fall. This way they can monitor where swans are breeding, where their stopover points are located, and when they start their annual migrations. Each spring the swans fly to Alaska and to the Canadian coast, near the Arctic Circle. They fly in a V-shaped formation and can travel up to 100 miles per hour.

eleven

11 tundra swans,
           wintering in North Carolina lakes—
     graceful, floating ballerinas,
           honking and calling as the day breaks.

Moravian hand-rolled cookies,
sugar, lemon, chocolate, and spice.
I'll take **12**, please.
The smell is so deliciously nice!

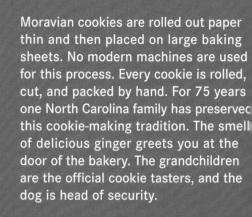

Moravian cookies are rolled out paper thin and then placed on large baking sheets. No modern machines are used for this process. Every cookie is rolled, cut, and packed by hand. For 75 years one North Carolina family has preserved this cookie-making tradition. The smell of delicious ginger greets you at the door of the bakery. The grandchildren are the official cookie tasters, and the dog is head of security.

The history of Moravian cookies in North Carolina goes back to the 1700s. The people from Moravia, Czechoslovakia, sought freedom in America. They settled at first in Pennsylvania and then a small band walked to Winston-Salem, North Carolina. The community of Clemmons, North Carolina, has a Moravian church that was built in 1773. Nine generations of the bakery families have attended the Moravian church and bake cookies from an original recipe. The cookies are so good with a big glass of cold milk, which is North Carolina's official state beverage.

twelve
12

13 quarts of strawberries,
one for my basket, two for my mouth.
13 pounds of blueberries.
It's berry-picking time in the South.

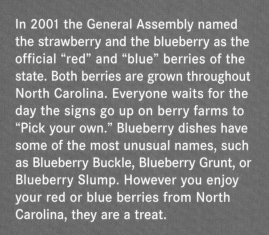

In 2001 the General Assembly named the strawberry and the blueberry as the official "red" and "blue" berries of the state. Both berries are grown throughout North Carolina. Everyone waits for the day the signs go up on berry farms to "Pick your own." Blueberry dishes have some of the most unusual names, such as Blueberry Buckle, Blueberry Grunt, or Blueberry Slump. However you enjoy your red or blue berries from North Carolina, they are a treat.

The strawberry is unique. It has 200 seeds, the only fruit with seeds found on the outside. From late April to May, strawberries are ready to be picked in our state. The American Indian was enjoying blueberries before the Pilgrims. They learned to preserve the berries by drying them and later added the berries to soups, stews, and meat.

thirteen
13

North Carolina's textile industry has a long history. From the early 1800s, industrialization brought mill workers, mill villages, mill stores, and mill schools to the state. Development of communities grew from this industry, and soon the villages grew into cities. Cotton mills sprang up along the banks of North Carolina's many rivers and canals. The water provided energy and steam for the plants. Later many mills converted to electricity. Cotton was called "white gold of the South."

Mill workers, often 12-year-old young boys, worked 12 to 14 hours a day. Sometimes all family members worked either in the cotton fields or in the mills. The pay was low, but families depended on the mills for their income. The mill owner built homes for the workers, and brought doctors and teachers to the villages.

Today many mills have closed. However, North Carolina can be proud of its textile design history and as the producer of fine towels, linens, clothing, and fabrics.

fourteen
14

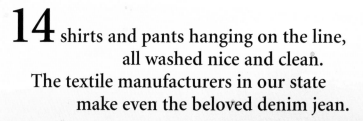

14 shirts and pants hanging on the line,
all washed nice and clean.
The textile manufacturers in our state
make even the beloved denim jean.

15 Scottish bagpipers
are elegantly clad.
Seen at Highland games,
in traditional plaid.

It is nighttime and the gathering of Scottish families at Grandfather Mountain Highland Games is quiet. Suddenly there is a wail in the background and then the wail becomes a skirl (high shrill tone). It is the Scottish Highland Pipers getting closer and closer. The audience breaks their silence with cheers and applauding.

The bagpiper stands regally in his or her uniform. The interlocking pattern of colored stripes woven into cloth is called plaid in America and tartan in Scotland. Each clan claims their own distinct tartan pattern that represents their family or location, but many times a tartan represents a good friend, or historical event. Whatever the reason, the tartan is worn with pride. Every year a meeting of Scots "summons the clans" to compete in the Highland Games. North Carolina has more residents of Scottish heritage than any other state in the United States. Therefore, a Scottish Tartans Museum was opened in North Carolina honoring its descendants.

fifteen
15

Waiting in a line
20 to tour the big ship.
smiling tourists,
on a special trip.

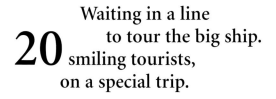

The USS *North Carolina* is moored (anchored) in Wilmington, North Carolina. Visitors go to visit this memorial honoring the men and women who served on the ship. The ship served in every major naval offense in the Pacific in World War II. It earned 15 battle stars for distinguished service and sailed home to Wilmington a hero.

The visit to the North Carolina ship is like a visit to a city. There were over 2,000 crew members that lived aboard the ship. The crew slept in metal bunks that were stacked five high. They could go to the movies, the bakery, and there was even a general store where they could buy things. The galley (kitchen) baked pumpkin pie for the holidays. The recipe called for 6 cases of pumpkin, 100 pounds of sugar, 30 gallons of water, 30 dozen eggs, and 22 pounds of cornstarch. How many eggs are in 30 dozen?

twenty

20

The Museum of Life and Science in Durham has a display of exotic insects, as well as native species from around the world. It is called the Aventis Crop Science Insectarium. Here visitors can see a collection of live and mounted insects. The live species include: giant orb weaver spiders, which are climbing freely along the upper exhibit walls and ceilings; monster walking sticks; a giant farm of harvester ants; and death head roaches with heads that resemble skulls. Entomologists (scientists who study insects) find new insect species daily. It is thought that there are more than 10 to 100 million insects to be discovered.

twenty-five

25

25 crawly, creepy, fascinating bugs,
some are mounted, some are alive.
Specimens from all over the world
they even have beehives!

30 whirlagigs—
large art pieces on display.
Movement and sounds welded from scraps
An outside museum tucked away.

Driving down a country road, we saw in the distance huge monster forms. As we drove closer, a tour bus was driving away. Visitors had been admiring one man's creative works.

In Wilson County, the Windmill Farm has a remarkable collection of whirligigs. An equally remarkable man, Vollis Simpson, has used his artistic ability to weld and paint huge pieces of metal into works of art. The 30 pieces are in constant movement with the breeze making whirring sounds. Mr. Simpson uses scraps of metal he finds and has become an environmentalist. Tucked away in a quiet farm setting, the art form he has created is truly unique.

thirty
30

North Carolina ranks seventh in the United States for apple production. Four major areas for apple orchards are Henderson, Haywood, Wilkes, and Cleveland counties. The four major varieties are Red Delicious, Golden Delicious, Rome Beauty, and Galas. However, other varieties are picked every year from mid-August through October. The old saying "An apple a day keeps the doctor away" is true. Apples are very rich in pectin and help fight many types of diseases.

Family recipes for apple pies, apple butter, fritters, apple cake, and apple cider have been handed down from one generation to another. At apple picking time, the older trees may each produce up to 20 bushels of apples a year. How many trees would produce 40 bushels of apples?

forty
40

40 bushels of apples,
Granny Smith and Red Delicious,
crispy, sweet-sour tangy flavor.
One a day is so nutritious.

50 Fraser fir trees
trimmed to perfection.
North Carolina's favorite Christmas tree,
waiting for selection.

The North Carolina Fraser fir tree has been judged in the United States as the best Christmas tree in a contest sponsored by the National Christmas Tree Association. It has been chosen for the official White House Christmas tree eight times. Fraser fir trees grow in the far western North Carolina counties. The state ranks second in the nation in number of trees harvested, Oregon being first.

It takes years of hard work to grow Christmas trees. The trees begin their life in a nursery. Seeds are taken from cones of mature trees, and then planted and covered with straw. After one year the seedling is still only the height of a quarter. When the seedlings are strong enough, they will be planted in a field. When the tree is seven to eight years old, it begins to have a tapered shape, with help from the grower. In nine to ten years, the tree will fill out and double in height. Finally, after 12 years of growth, the Fraser fir is seven to ten feet tall and ready to be harvested.

fifty
50

North Carolina has exactly 100 counties. From the coast to the heartland (Piedmont) and to the mountains, each county has its own distinct geographic areas. The coast is warmed by the gulf stream with beautiful beaches, giant sand dunes, and wetlands filled with wildlife and plants. The heartland is the central part of the state. Rolling foothills, moderate weather, and our state's capital, Raleigh, are found here. The mountains have the Appalachian chain that runs through the western part of the state. Here is the Blue Ridge Parkway and magnificent views of Mount Mitchell, the tallest mountain on the East Coast. Raleigh, Greensboro, Durham, Winston-Salem, and Fayetteville follow Charlotte, our largest city.

Which county do you live in? Did you know each county has its own newspaper? What is the name of your newspaper? Have fun with 100!

one
hundred
100

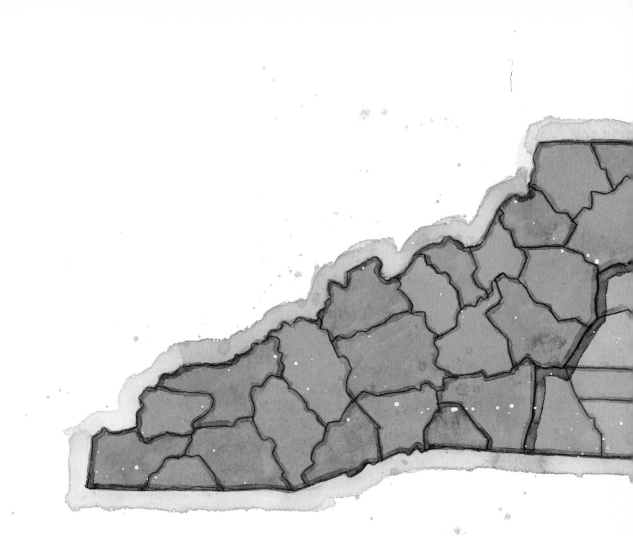

Can you find the counties? **100** in this state.
There are **100** in this state.
From Alamance to Yancy
each one is first rate.

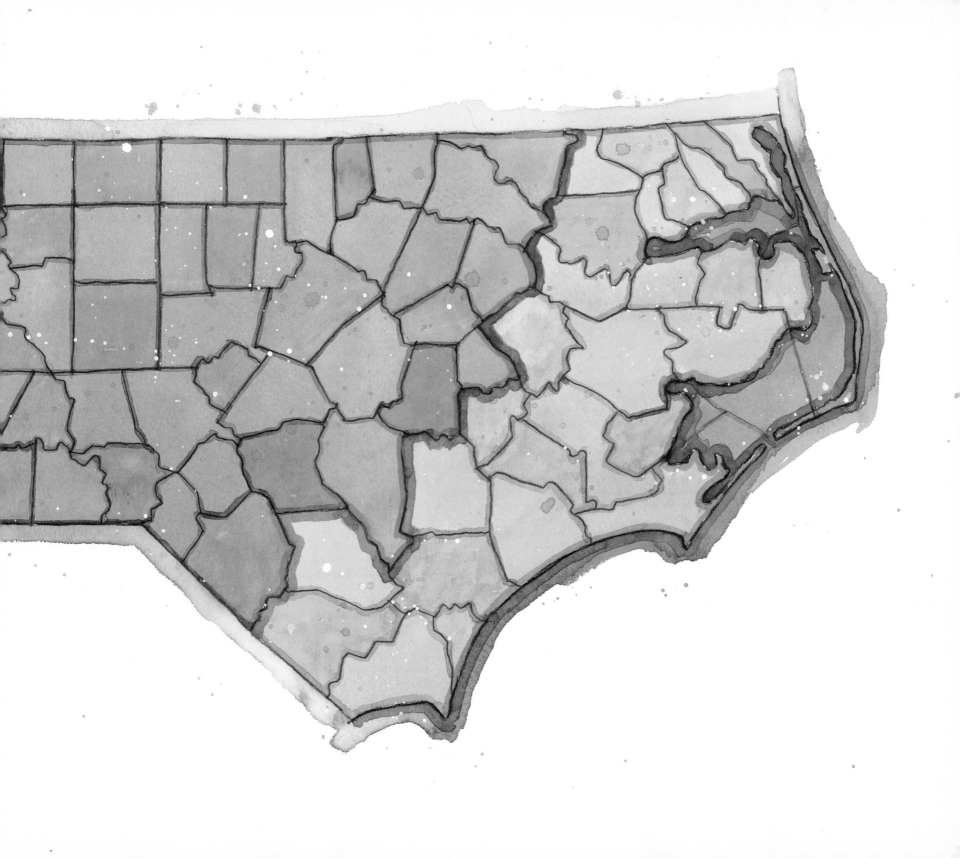

Carol Crane

Carol Crane is honored to return to North Carolina where she and her husband now reside in Holly Springs. She has also written *Sunny Numbers: A Florida Counting Book* and *Round Up: A Texas Number Book*, as well as alphabet books for Florida, Texas, Alaska, Georgia, South Carolina, North Carolina, Alabama, and Delaware.

Carol is a historian and has always been a journal writer. Traveling around the country, she speaks at reading conventions and schools, networking with children and educators on the fabric that makes up the quilt of this great country. Her greatest joy is to have a child say, "Wow! I didn't know that."

Gary Palmer

Gary Palmer, born in Alabama to a military family, was raised all over the country and in Europe. He began showing an interest in drawing as early as five years of age. Some of his most rewarding projects have been those that showcase the natural beauty of North Carolina. This is Gary's second book with Sleeping Bear Press, and another opportunity to get out and explore the interesting people and places of North Carolina. Gary lives in Charlotte with his wife Rebecca and sons, Joel and Evan.